THE POCKET SPELL CREATOR

Magickal References at Your Fingertips

By
Kerri Connor

NEW PAGE BOOKS
A division of The Career Press, Inc.
Franklin Lakes, NJ

THE POCKET SPELL CREATOR

EDITED AND TYPESET BY NICOLE DEFELICE

Cover design by Cheryl Cohan Finbow
Illustrated by Kate Paddock
Printed in the U.S.A. by Book-mart Press

To order this title, please call toll-free 1-800-CAREER-1 (NJ and Canada: 201-848-0310) to order using VISA or MasterCard, or for further information on books from Career Press.

The Career Press, Inc., 3 Tice Road, PO Box 687,
Franklin Lakes, NJ 07417
www.careerpress.com
www.newpagebooks.com

CAREER PRESS

New Page BOOKS

Library of Congress Cataloging-in-Publication Data

Connor, Kerri, 1970-
    The pocket spell creator : magickal references at your fingertips / by
Kerri Connor.
        p. cm.
    Includes bibliographical references and index.
    ISBN 1-56414-715-0 (pbk.)
        1. Magic—Handbooks, manuals, etc. I. Title.

BF1611.C724 2003
133.4'4—dc22

2003059999

Dedicated to Wendy Woo,
Ye Olde Penguin

Disclaimer

The herbal information in this book is provided for educational purpose only and is not meant to be used without consulting a qualified health practitioner before use. Please contact your physician before ingesting or applying anything to your skin.

Contents

Introduction

This book is designed to help you make up your own spells and find which ones and what type work best for you.

The book is divided into multiple sections, so you may choose a selection from each topic to create your final spell. This book is best used for browsing instead of reading straight through. Find what you need from each section to create your spells. At the end there are worksheet examples you can use to record your own spells and rituals along with their results so that you may look back and see what has had positive results for you, and also what hasn't.

To get started, skim through the entire book and familiarize yourself with the worksheets and the different sections.

Section 1

The Elements and Their Associations

Earth

Direction: North.

Zodiac Signs: Taurus, Virgo, Capricorn.

Practical, skillful, down-to-earth, deals with physical things and financial matters.

Rules: Body, growth, nature, sustenance, material gain, prosperity, money, death, caverns, fields, meadows, plants, trees, animals, rocks, crystals, manifestations, and materialization.

Time: Midnight.

Season: Winter.

Colors: Black, brown, green, gold, mustard.

Oils: Pine, cypress, cedar, sage, vetivert.

Air

Direction: East.

Zodiac Signs: Gemini, Libra, Aquarius.

Social, intellectual, concerned with ideas, communication, and social interrelationships.

Rules: The mind, all mental, intellectual, and some psychic work, knowledge, abstract thought, theory, mountaintops, prairies open to the wind, wind, breath, clouds, vapor and mist, storms, purification, removal of stagnation, new beginnings.

Time: Dawn.

Season: Spring.

Colors: White, yellow, lavender, pale blue, grey.

Oils: Frankincense, violet, lavender, lemon, rosemary.

Water

Direction: West.

Zodiac Signs: Cancer, Scorpio, Pisces.

Sensitive, emotional, intuitive, romantic, seem to think with their emotions.

Rules: Emotions, feelings, love, sorrow, intuition, the subconscious, conscious mind, womb, fertility, menstruation, cleansing, purification, ocean, lakes, tide pools, springs, wells.

Time: Twilight.

Season: Autumn.

Colors: Blue, blue-green, grey, aquamarine, indigo, white.

Oils: Lemon, lily of the valley, camphor.

Fire

Direction: South.

Zodiac Signs: Aries, Leo, Sagittarius.

Energetic, idealistic, assertive, courageous, active, stimulating, creative, and passionate.

Rules: Creativity, passion, energy, blood, healing, destruction, temper, faerie fire, phosphorescence, will-'o-the-wisps, volcanoes, flame, lava, bonfires, deserts, the sun.

Time: Noon.

Season: Summer.

Colors: Red, orange, gold, crimson, white, peridot.

Oils: Lime, orange, neroli, citronella.

Section 2

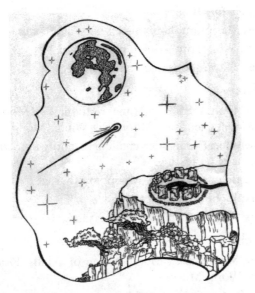

Full Moons and Their Associations

January

Wolf Moon, Quiet Moon, Snow Moon.

Do spells for: Beginnings.

Herbs: Marjoram, holy thistle, nuts, and cones.

Colors: White, blue-violet, black.

Stones: Garnet, onyx, jet, chrysoprase.

February

Storm Moon, Ice Moon, Hunger Moon, Wild Moon, Red Moon, Cleansing Moon, Big Winter Moon.

Do spells for: Facing life's challenges, purifying, dedicating or rededicating.

Herbs: Balm of Gilead, hyssop, myrrh, sage.

Colors: Light blue, violet.

Stones: Amethyst, jasper, rock crystal.

March

Chaste Moon, Seed Moon, Moon of Winds, Plow Moon, Worm Moon.

Do spells for: Success and hope.

Herbs: Irish moss.

Colors: Green, violet.

Stones: Aquamarine, bloodstone.

April

Seed Moon, Growing Moon, Planting Moon, Pink Moon, Green Grass Moon.

Do spells for: Planting.

Herbs: Basil, chives, dragon's blood, geranium, thistle.

Colors: Red, gold.

Stones: Ruby, garnet.

May

Hare Moon, Merry Moon, Flower Moon.

Do spells for: Health, love, romance, wisdom.

Herbs: Elder, mint, rose, mugwort, thyme, yarrow.

Colors: Green, brown, pink.

Stones: Emerald, malachite, amber.

June

Lovers Moon, Mead Moon, Honey Moon, Rose Moon, Strawberry Moon.

Do spells for: Romance, sex.

Herbs: Skullcap, meadowsweet, parsley.

Colors: Orange, yellow-green.

Stones: Topaz, agate, alexandrite.

July

Mead Moon, Hay Moon, Wort Moon, Moon of Blood, Thunder Moon.

Do spells for: Enchantment, health, success, strength.

Herbs: Honeysuckle, lemon balm, hyssop.

Colors: Silver, blue-grey.

Stones: Pearl, moonstone, white agate.

August

Wyrt Moon, Corn Moon, Barley Moon, Harvest Moon.

Do spells for: Abundance, plants, agriculture, herbs, marriage.

Herbs: Chamomile, St. John's wort, bay, angelica, fennel, rue, orange.

Colors: Yellow, gold.

Stones: Cat's-eye, jasper, fire agate.

September

Harvest Moon, Wine Moon, Singing Moon.

Do spells for: Protection, prosperity, abundance.

Herbs: Copal, fennel, rye, wheat, valerian, skullcap.

Colors: Brown, yellow-green, yellow.

Stones: Peridot, olivine, chrysolite, citrine.

October

Blood Moon, Harvest Moon, Moon of the Changing Season.

Do spells for: New goals, protection, spirituality, resolution.

Herbs: Pennyroyal, thyme, catnip, angelica, burdock.

Colors: Dark blue-green.

Stones: Opal, tourmaline, turquoise.

November

Snow Moon, Dark Moon, Fog Moon, Mourning Moon, Mad Moon.

Do spells for: Family, friends, divination.

Herbs: Verbena, thistle.

Colors: Grey, sea green.

Stones: Topaz, lapis lazuli.

December

Oak Moon, Cold Moon, Wolf Moon, Moon of Long Nights.

Do spells for: Hope and healing.

Herbs: Holly, English ivy, fir, mistletoe.

Colors: Red, white, black.

Stones: Serpentine, peridot.

Section 3

Moon Phases and Their Associations

New Moon

When the moon is not visible.

Banishments, psychic energy, healing, resting.

Waxing Crescent Moon

When the visible part of the moon is less than half full and increasing.

Invoke things you want, start new projects, control energies and growth.

First Quarter

When half of the moon is full and increasing.

Full Moon

When the full moon is visible.

Integrating and perfecting ideas and projects, working on positives, psychic energy, creativity, physical energy.

Last Quarter

When half of the moon is full and decreasing.

Waning Crescent Moon

When the visible part of the moon is less than half full and decreasing.

Section 4

Days of the Week and Their Associations

Sunday

Ruled by the sun.

Success, power, swift change, God ritual, healing, spirituality, strength, and protection.

Monday

Ruled by the moon.

Psychic work, Goddess ritual, faerie magick, peace, sleep, healing, compassion, friends, purification, and fertility.

Tuesday

Ruled by Mars.

Protection, victory, courage, athletics, passion, sex, and aggression.

Wednesday

Ruled by Mercury.

Communication, intellectual pursuits, flexibility, the conscious mind, study, travel, and wisdom.

Thursday

Ruled by Jupiter.

Business, group pursuits, joy, laughter, expansion, money, prosperity, and generosity.

Friday

Ruled by Venus.

Love, friendship, nature, beauty, arts and crafts, and reconciliation.

Saturday

Ruled by Saturn.

Crystallization, hidden or obscured matters, limitations and boundaries, longevity, exorcisms, endings, homes and houses.

Section 5

Colors and Their Associations

Black

Divination, banishing, absorption of negative energy, protection, binding, limitations, loss, confusion, defining boundaries.

Blue

Truth, tranquility, protection, hope, honor, change, psychic abilities, sleep, dreams, peace, healing, fidelity, unity, astral projection, virgin goddesses, wisdom, knowledge.

Brown

Stability, integrity, justice, sensuality, endurance, animals, concentration, grounding, earth, neutrality, strength, grace, decision-making, pets, family issues.

Gold

The God, vitality, strength, success, action, courage, confidence, solar deities, summer, wealth, employment, masculinity, sun, power, daylight hours.

Grey

Vision, neutrality, absorption negativity, anger, greed, envy.

Green
Abundance, growth, healing, prosperity, fertility, employment, luck, jealousy, personal appearance, neutralizes difficult situations, calming, finances, security, career.

Indigo
Insight, vision, change, flexibility, psychic abilities.

Light blue
Calmness, tranquility, patience, understanding, good health.

Magenta
Intuition, change, spiritual healing, vitality.

Orange
Courage, pride, ambition, enthusiasm, energy, friendship, communication, success, opportunities, attraction, willpower, sun, adaptability, zest for life, imagination.

Pink
Compassion, tenderness, harmony, affection, love, romance, spiritual healing, spring, household peace, honor, virtue, morality, success, contentment.

Purple

Growth, self-esteem, psychic ability, insight, inspiration, spirituality, success in business, power, mild banishings, ambition, inner strength, physical fitness.

Red

Sexual love, lust, passion, fire, willpower, courage, energy, strength, anger, blood, life cycle, desire, war.

Silver

The Goddess, spiritual truth, intuition, receptivity, psychic ability, stability, balance, moon, inner self, spells of femininity, moon power, night.

Turquoise

Creativity, discipline, self-knowledge, honor, idealism.

Violet

Success, intuition, self-improvement, spiritual awareness, deep sleep, healing.

White

Cleansing, peace, protection, healing, truth, divination, tranquility, purification, childhood, innocence.

Yellow

Joy, vitality, intelligence, study, persuasion, charm, creativity, communication, mind power, sun, psychic ability, attraction, examinations and tests.

Section 6

Crystals and Stones and Their Associations

Agate

Courage, strength, love, protection.

Alexandrite

Luck, love, spiritual transformation, joy.

Amazonite

Success, joy, self-expression.

Amethyst

Courage, psychic energy, dreams, healing addictions, peace, happiness, love.

Aquamarine

Courage, purification, peace, psychic awareness, self-expression.

Aventurine

Money, luck, mental agility, visual acuity, peace, healing.

Azurite

Psychic energy, dreams, divination, healing, concentration, transformation.

Beryl

Energy, love, healing, psychic awareness, protection.

Bloodstone

Courage, strength, victory, wealth, self-confidence, business and legal affairs.

Calcite

Centering, grounding, purification, money, peace, calms fears.

Carnelian

Courage, sexual energy, verbal skills, peace, stops jealousy, stops apathy, stops fear and rage.

Celestite

Verbal skills, healing, compassion, calming, aids growth.

Chrysocolla

Wisdom, peace, love, communication, vitality.

Chrysoprase

Prosperity, luck, happiness, friendship, protection, healing.

Citrine

Psychic powers, protection, creativity, sexual energy, prevents nightmares.

Clear quartz

Intensifies energy.

Diamond

Courage, strength, healing, protection, spirituality, mental and sexual abilities.

Emerald

Prosperity, mental and psychic abilities, dreams, meditation, visual acuity, love, peace, balance.

Garnet

Strength, physical energy, healing, protection, purification, compassion.

Geode

Fertility, childbirth, meditation, freedom of spirit, psychic ability, dreams, astral travel.

Hematite
Grounding, calming, healing, divination, intuition, physical strength, aids restful sleep.

Jade
Healing, protection, wisdom, prosperity, love, long life, fertility, courage, peace.

Jasper
Healing, protection, health, beauty, energy.

Kunzite
Creativity, communication, peace, balance, relaxation, grounding.

Lapis lazuli
Courage, joy, love, fidelity, psychic abilities, protection, healing, beauty, prosperity.

Lepidolite
Peace, spirituality, physical strength, luck, protection, psychic ability, emotional balance, prevents nightmares.

Malachite
Power, energy, protection, love, peace, success in business, vision quests, gardening.

Moldavite

Psychic abilities, mental and emotional balance.

Moonstone

Grounding, love, divination, sleep, gardening, protection, youth, harmony, peace, travel.

Obsidian

Grounding, divination, protection, prevents negativity.

Onyx

Emotional balance, self-control, binding, protection, strength.

Opal

Beauty, prosperity, luck, power, psychic abilities, visual acuity, emotional balance.

Peridot

Protection, prosperity, sleep, health, emotional balance, intuition.

Rhodochrosite

Energy, peace, calm, love, mental activity, emotional balance.

Rhodonite

Peace, mental clarity, memory, confidence.

Rose quartz

Love, peace, happiness, healing.

Ruby

Prosperity, power, courage, integrity, joy, prevents nightmares.

Sapphire

Psychic abilities, inspiration, love, meditation, peace, healing, power, prosperity, protection.

Smokey quartz

Healing, directing and absorbing energy, altered states.

Sodalite

Healing, meditation, wisdom, calm, grounding, stress reducer.

Sunstone

Protection, energy, health, passion, sexuality.

Tiger's-eye

Courage, prosperity, protection, energy, luck, judgment, common sense, honesty, divination, eases depression.

Topaz

Protection, healing, dieting, prosperity, love, emotional balance, tranquility, creativity.

Tourmaline

Love, friendship, prosperity, business, peace, sleep, energy, courage, protection, inspiration.

Turquoise

Courage, protection, prosperity, luck, friendship, healing, communication, happiness, emotional balance, astral travel.

Zircon

Protection, beauty, love, peace, sexual energy, healing, mental alertness, emotional balance.

Section 7

Foods and Their Associations

Almonds
Money, wisdom.

Apples
Attract love, heal, aid in divination.

Avocados
Love, lust.

Bananas
Fertility, potency, prosperity.

Barley
Love, healing, protection.

Beets
Love.

Blackberries
Healing, prosperity, money.

Carrots
Fertility, lust.

Cashews
Money.

Celery
Mental and psychic powers.

Corn
Protection, luck, divination.

Cucumbers
Healing, fertility.

Grapes
Fertility, mental powers.

Leeks
Protection, love.

Lemons
Purification, mental clarity.

Mustard
Mental powers, fertility.

Oranges
Prosperity, luck.

Pineapples
Love, money.

Pomegranates
Divination, wealth.

Rice
Rain, fertility, money.

Strawberries
Love, luck.

Turnips
Protection, help end relationships.

Vanilla
Attracts men, promotes mental energy.

Section 8

Herbs and Plants and Their Associations

Acacia

Protection, psychic powers.

Alder

Divination and scrying, support, foundation, magickal beginnings, fire and water magick.

Allspice

Money, luck, healing.

Almond

Money, prosperity, wisdom.

Amber

Stability, self-confidence, peace.

Ambergris

Awakens love and emotion.

Angelica

Protection, healing, visions, removes hexes, cleansing, purification, exorcism.

Anise

Protection, purification, youth.

Apple (wood)
Love, initiation, fertility, spiritual contact.

Apple blossom
Love, friendship, celebrating life cycles, peace.

Aspen (wood)
Invoke magickal shields, protection, healing.

Balm of Gilead
Love, manifestations, protection, emotional healing.

Basil
Happiness, peace, money.

Bay (wood)
Protection, healing, divination.

Bayberry
Money, good luck, peace, harmony, well-being.

Bay Leaves
Psychic awareness, purification.

Beech (wood)
Knowledge.

Benzoin
Purification, prosperity, magickal energy, conscious mind.

Bergamot
Money, peace, happiness, restful sleep, breaks hexes.

Bergamot mint
Physical energy, prosperity.

Birch (wood)
Fertility, purification, banishment of negativity.

Black pepper
Mental alertness, physical energy, protection, courage.

Blackthorn (wood)
Protection.

Blessed thistle
Purification, protection, breaks hexes.

Bluebell
Constancy, strength, luck, truth.

Bramble (wood)
Healing.

Buckeye
Attracts money, stops aches and pains.

Buckthorn (wood)
Healing.

Burdock
Protection, healing, happy home.

Buttercup
Prosperity, happiness.

Calendula
Health, psychic dreams, comfort.

Camellia
Gratitude, prosperity.

Camphor
Awakens memories, psychic awareness, purification, physical energy, celibacy.

Caraway

Conscious mind, physical energy, love.

Cardamom

Love, sex.

Carnation

Protection, strength, healing, vitality, physical energy, love, health, magickal energy.

Catnip

Psychic bond with cats, attracts good spirits, love, luck, peace, beauty.

Cedar

Healing, courage, purification, protection, money, hex-breaking, spirituality, self-control.

Celery seeds

Lust, mental and psychic powers, sleep.

Cereus

Psychic awareness.

Chamomile
Sleep, meditation, money, peace.

Cherry
Divination, love.

Cinnamon
Lust, love, success, power, psychic awareness, physical energy, prosperity.

Clove
Money, lust, love, exorcism, protection, courage, healing, memory.

Clover
Protection, money, love, fidelity, success, exorcism.

Coffee
Conscious mind.

Coltsfoot
Peace, tranquility, visions, animal spells.

Columbine
Courage, willpower.

Comfrey
Safe travel, money.

Copal
Purification.

Coriander
Memory, love, healing.

Costmary
Conscious mind, stilling emotions, purification.

Cowslip
Attracts spring faeries, wealth, health, keeps others away (when you want to be alone—not for banishing).

Crocus
Attracts love.

Cumin
Protection.

Cyclamen
Love and truth.

Cypress

Comfort, solace, eases feelings of loss, healing.

Daffodil

Honors Gods and Goddesses of spring, fertility, wishing, love.

Daisy

Attracts love and lust.

Damiana

Lust, love.

Dandelion

Divination, calling spirits, favorable winds.

Deer's-tongue

Psychic awareness.

Dill

Money, love, lust, protection, conscious mind, purification.

Dragon's blood

Power amplifier, protection, love, banishing, potency.

Elder (wood)

Faerie contact, healing, summoning spirits.

Elderberry

Prosperity, protection, sleep, banishing of negative entities.

Elm (wood)

Rites of the Goddess, feminine magick.

Eucalyptus

Healing, protection, purification.

Fennel

Longevity, courage, purification.

Fenugreek

Money, mental powers.

Frankincense

Spirituality, protection, banishing of negative entities, consecration, meditation.

Freesia

Love, peace.

Galangal

Magickal energy, protection.

Gardenia

Love, peace, healing, enhances spiritual connections.

Garlic

Protection, purification, health, physical energy, conscious mind.

Geranium

Fertility, health, protection, love, happiness.

Ginger

Success, power, money, love, magickal energy, physical energy, sex, courage.

Ginseng

Love, lust, vitality, wishes, healing, beauty, protection, luck.

Gota kola

Meditation.

Hawthorn

Attracts faeries, protection, invoke a psychic shield.

Heliotrope
Money, gain power.

Hemlock
Astral projection.

Hibiscus
Love, lust, divination.

Holly
Rites of male magick, warrior magick, protection from negative forces.

Honeysuckle
Money, psychic awareness, memory, healing, honesty and mental powers, weight loss, prosperity.

Hops
Healing, sleep.

Horehound
Protection, healing, mental powers, banishing of negative entities.

Hyacinth
Love, protection, happiness, overcoming grief, peaceful sleep.

Hyssop
Purification, protection, prosperity, conscious mind.

Iris
Love, psychic awareness.

Irish moss
Money, luck, safe travel.

Ivy
Binding magick, protection from psychic attack.

Jasmine
Love, money, sleep, dreams, peace, spirituality, sex.

John the conqueror
Money, love, happiness, hex-breaking, protection.

Juniper
Protection, love, health, banishing of negative entities, exorcism, purification.

Lavender
Happiness, healing, peace, sleep, purification, love, celibacy, conscious mind.

Lemon

Health, healing, physical energy, purification.

Lemon balm

Peace, money, purification.

Lemon grass

Psychic awareness, purification.

Lemon verbena

Love, purification.

Lilac

Protection, beauty, love, helps reveal past lives, purification.

Lily

Protection, purity, breaking love spells, peace, eases pain of ended relationships.

Lily of the valley

Happiness, mental powers, conscious mind, peace, memory.

Lime

Purification, physical energy, protection.

Linden (wood)
Feminine power, rites of the Goddess.

Lotus
Spirituality, love, protection.

Mace
Psychic awareness.

Magnolia
Peace, nature spells, love.

Mandrake
Protection, fertility, love, money.

Maple (wood)
Rituals of celebration.

Marigold
Protection, dreams, psychic powers, business.

Marjoram
Peace, celibacy, sleep.

Meadowsweet
Peace, love.

Melon

Healing, health.

Mimosa

Psychic dreams, love.

Mistletoe

Protection, love, fertility, health, exorcism, luck, healing, good fortune.

Mugwort

Divination, clairvoyance, psychic powers, dreams, protection, strength, astral projection.

Mullein

Courage, love, divination, protection.

Musk

Courage, fertility, lust.

Mustard

Fertility, money, protection, mental acuity.

Myrrh

Spirituality, healing, protection, exorcism, transformation, consecration, meditation.

Narcissus
Peace, harmony, love.

Nasturtium
Physical energy, protection.

Neroli
Purification, joy, sex.

Nettle
Protection, healing, lust, banishing negative entities.

Niaouli
Protection, healing.

Nutmeg
Fidelity, luck, money, love, physical energy, magickal energy, psychic awareness.

Oak (wood)
Protection, midsummer, divination, spiritual contact.

Oakmoss
Money.

Onion

Courage, protection.

Orange

Divination, love, luck, money, joy, purification, physical energy, magickal energy.

Orange blossom

Beauty, love, marriage.

Orris

Long-lasting love, divination, protection.

Palmarosa

Love, healing.

Parsley

Purification, protection, lust, fertility.

Passionflower

Peace, friendship, popularity, sleep.

Patchouli

Fertility, lust, money, protection, divination, sex, physical energy.

Pennyroyal

Protection, peace, strength, anti-seasickness, physical energy, conscious mind.

Peppermint

Love, psychic awareness, lust, mental stimulant, energy, purification.

Periwinkle

Love, lust, money, protection.

Petitgrain

Conscious mind, protection.

Pine

Healing, protection, fertility, money, banishing negative entities, knowledge, fire magick, illumination, purification, physical energy, magickal energy.

Plumeria

Love, peace.

Poplar (wood)

Divination.

Poppy

Fertility, love, money, luck, sleep.

Primrose

Love, protection, attracts highly sexual love, attracts spring faeries.

Raspberry

Love, home protection, alleviates labor pains.

Rhododendron

Peace, strength.

Rose

Love, beauty, luck, psychic powers, protection, peace, sex.

Rose geranium

Protection, fertility, love, health.

Rosemary

Mental powers, youth, protection, love, lust, purification, sleep, exorcism, longevity, conscious mind, memory, love.

Rowan (wood)

Protection, divination.

Rue

Healing, mental powers, protection, love, calms emotions.

Saffron

Conscious mind, physical energy, magickal energy, money.

Sage

Wisdom, prosperity, healing, longevity, money, memory, conscious mind.

Sandalwood

Spirituality, protection, wishes, healing, exorcism, meditation, sex.

Sassafras

Health, money.

Slippery elm

Stops gossip, aids verbal development.

Snapdragon
Protection, friendship.

Spearmint
Healing, love, mental powers, protection during sleep.

Spider lily
Love, peace.

Spikenard
Good luck, fidelity, health.

Star anise
Psychic and spiritual powers, luck.

Stephanotis
Love, peace.

Strawberry
Love, luck, beauty.

Sunflower
Wisdom, health, fertility, wish realization.

Sweet pea
Friendship, courage, strength, happiness.

Tangerine
Psychic and mental powers.

Tea tree
Healing, antifungal.

Thyme
Courage, conscious mind, health.

Tonka bean
Love, money, courage, wishes.

Tuberose
Peace, love.

Tulip
Love, happiness, dreams, purification.

Valerian
Love, sleep, purification, protection, peace.

Vanilla
Mental powers, love, lust, sex, physical and magickal energy.

Vervain

Love, protection, purification, peace, money, youth, healing.

Vetivert

Love, luck, money, protection against theft.

Violet

Spiritual protection, luck, love, lust, wishes, peace, sleep, healing.

Water lily

Peace, happiness, love.

Whitebeam (wood)

Earth magick.

Willow

Love, divination, protection, healing, rebirth, purification, feminine magick.

Witch hazel

Protection, chastity, healing a broken heart.

Wood aloe
Spirituality, meditation, love.

Woodruff
Success, purification.

Wormwood
Psychic powers, protection, safe car travel, love, calling spirits.

Yarrow
Courage, protection, love, psychic powers.

Yerba santa
Beauty, healing, psychic powers, protection.

Yew (wood)
Initiation, funeral rites.

Ylang-ylang
Love, lust, peace, sex.

Zinnia
Love, lust, strength.

Section 9

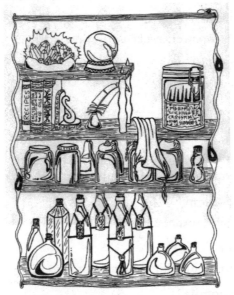

Oils and Their Associations

Basil

Money, harmony, promotes sympathy, happiness, peace.

Benison

Increases power, awakens the conscious mind, peace.

Bergamot

Money, protection.

Black pepper

Protection, courage, banishing, spices up romance.

Camphor

Purification, healing, chastity.

Cardamom

Love, lust, sexual energy.

Cedar

Balance, spirituality, courage, dreams.

Chamomile

Mediation, peace, dreams.

Cinnamon

Money, psychic awareness, lust, purification.

Clove
Courage, protection, sexual attractiveness, lust, adds spice to any situation.

Coriander
Love, health, healing.

Cypress
Consecration, protection, healing, longevity.

Eucalyptus
Health, healing, purification.

Ginger
Sexuality, love, courage, money, prosperity.

Grapefruit
Purification, banishes a sour disposition.

Jasmine
Love, psychic awareness, dreams, peace, sex.

Juniper
Protection, meditation, purification, healing, and communication.

Lavender
Health, peace, relaxation, sleep, purification, love.

Lemon
Energy, mental clarity, cleansing.

Lemon grass
Psychic awareness, purification, lust.

Lemon verbena
Love, purification.

Lime
Purification, cleansing, protection, fertility, love.

Magnolia
Meditation, psychic awareness, love, fidelity.

Myrrh
Spirituality, meditation, healing, blessing.

Neroli
Happiness, protection, purification.

Oakmoss
Money, prosperity, fertility.

Orange
Purification, heightened awareness, luck.

Palmarosa
Love, healing, protection.

Patchouli
Money, physical energy, attraction, protection, sex.

Peppermint
Purification, mental energy, psychic powers.

Pine
Purification, money, healing, cleansing.

Rose
Love, peace, sexual desire, beauty, maternal love.

Rosemary
Love, healing, energy, breaks hexes.

Sandalwood
Spirituality, meditation, sex, healing, psychic awareness.

Sweet pea
New friends, love, happiness.

Tangerine

Strength, power, vitality.

Tuberose

Calm, peace, love, happiness, psychic powers.

Vetivert

Money, prosperity, attractiveness, breaks hexes.

Yarrow

Courage, love, psychic awareness, banishes negative entities.

Ylang-ylang

Love, peace, sex, healing.

Section 10

Types of Spells

Candle spells

A colored candle

A pointed crystal

Oil

Mortar and pestle (optional to grind herbs)

Candle holder

Use crystal to carve desire on candle.

Rub oil on candle. Rub towards yourself from wick to end to bring something to you. Rub away from you end to wick to push something away.

Incense spells

Incense

Incense burner

Matches or lighter

Charcoal

Potion spells

Boil herbs in water for 10 minutes while covered. Strain herbs out of water and use potion as intended.

Do not take anything internally that may be harmful!

Powder spells

Mix herbs and grind into powder.

Powder can be blown, buried, sprinkled, or used in other ways as needed.

Flower spells

Dry flowers.
Grind.

Use as needed, whether as an incense ingredient, to burn alone, add to a bath, boil for the scent, or for use in an Air/wind spell where the ground flowers are thrown into a breeze. Use dried flowers that correspond with your needs.

Bath spells

Bath salts

Accompany with corresponding colored candle and incense (see Sections 5 and 12).

Full Moon water

Place a glass jar of water under the Full Moon. Ask your Goddess to bless the water with her light and love.

Use whenever your spells call for water.

Replenish your supply each month and pour the leftover water from the previous month into your garden, plants, or lawn—never down the drain!

Section 11

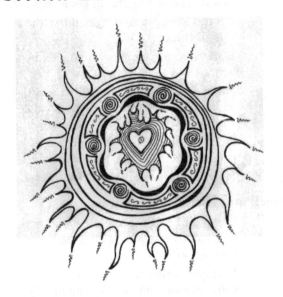

Ethics and Procedures

Spell and Ritual Ethics

1. Always follow the "harm none" rule.
2. Always observe and remember the rule of three.
3. Reinforce all spells with your daily actions.
4. Always make sure you realize exactly what it is you want and state your wishes descriptively and accurately.
5. Do not cast spells on other people, especially when they don't know about it!
6. Help others in their spiritual journeys.

Spell and Ritual Procedures

1. Clean and prepare the area you will be using to cast your spell or perform your ritual.
2. Prepare yourself—mentally, physically, emotionally, and spiritually.
3. Set up your altar with the needed items.
4. Cast your circle.
5. Invoke the elements.

6. Invoke any deities you are going to work with.
7. Perform the spell or ritual.
8. Thank the deities.
9. Dismiss the elements.
10. Open the circle.

Section 12

Oil, Incense, and Bath Salts Recipes

Most of these recipes can be converted between oils, incense, and bath salts. Just pick the form you are most comfortable using and mix it accordingly. Of course, the herbs and/or plants must be available in oil form to combine them for oils or bath salts. Drops of oil can be converted to parts for dry materials.

OILS

Business Success Oil 1

2 drops benison
2 drops lemon
2 drops magnolia
2 drops patchouli

Business Success Oil 2

2 drops John the conqueror
2 drops clover
2 drops balm of Gilead
2 drops bergamot

Business Success Oil 3

2 drops tangerine
3 drops vetivert

5 drops yarrow

3 drops patchouli

Business Success Oil 4

4 drops sweet pea

5 drops ginger

2 drops sage

2 drops basil

2 drops bergamot

Business Success Oil 5

3 drops cypress

4 drops cedar

4 drops sweet pea

2 drops cinnamon

Business Success Oil 6

6 drops cinnamon

5 drops cypress

4 drops ginger

3 drops sweet pea

2 drops sage

Business Success Oil 7

4 drops chamomile
3 drops cedar
2 drops basil

Business Success Oil 8

6 drops vetivert
4 drops cypress
3 drops ginger

Business Success Oil 9

6 drops lemon
4 drops sage
3 drops ginger

Business Success Oil 10

2 drops juniper
2 drops cedar
2 drops ginger
2 drops basil
2 drops cypress
2 drops lemon
2 drops sage

Love Oil 1

2 drops bergamot
2 drops damiana
2 drops jasmine
2 drops rose

Love Oil 2

2 drops cinnamon
2 drops clove
2 drops rosemary

Love Oil 3

2 drops camphor
2 drops damiana
2 drops sweet pea

Love Oil 4

2 drops bay
2 drops jasmine

Love Oil 5

2 drops jasmine
2 drops rosemary
2 drops sweet pea

Love Oil 6 (for men's use)

1/2 cup apricot
3 drops cinnamon
4 drops patchouli
2 drops rosemary
4 drops sandalwood

Love Oil 7

4 drops cinnamon
1 drop patchouli
3 drops rose
4 drops sandalwood

Love Oil 8

10 drops jasmine
5 drops lilac
5 drops lotus
2 drops rose
4 drops violet

Love Oil 9

7 drops carnation
5 drops geranium

2 drops jasmine
1 drop lilac
1 drop orange
2 drops rose
2 drops violet

Love Oil 10

5 drops carnation
5 drops hibiscus
10 drops honeysuckle
8 drops poppy
10 drops rose

Love Oil 11

10 drops carnation
5 drops citronella
10 drops geranium
5 drops orange

Love Oil 12

5 drops jasmine
3 drops lavender
2 drops rose

Money Oil 1

8 drops dill
13 drops bergamot
21 drops nutmeg
9 drops tonka
6 drops clove

Money Oil 2

20 drops chamomile
20 drops cedar
20 drops patchouli
13 drops clove

Money Oil 3

21 drops patchouli
14 drops chamomile
7 drops cinnamon
7 drops cedar

Money Oil 4

3 drops basil
3 drops bergamot
3 drops cinnamon

Money Oil 5

4 drops oakmoss
5 drops vetivert
3 drops basil

Money Oil 6

5 drops patchouli
7 drops ginger
2 drops basil
5 drops bergamot
3 drops cinnamon

Money Oil 7

7 drops ginger
7 drops cinnamon
2 drops basil
2 drops bergamot

Money Oil 8

3 drops oakmoss
3 drops basil
3 drops bergamot
3 drops sage

Money Oil 9

5 drops sage
5 drops vetivert
3 drops ginger

Money Oil 10

5 drops patchouli
3 drops basil
2 drops sage
2 drops vetivert

Money Oil 11

2 drops sage
2 drops basil
2 drops bergamot

Money Oil 12

3 drops basil
3 drops bergamot
3 drops cinnamon
3 drops oakmoss
3 drops patchouli

3 drops vetivert

3 drops sage

Muscle Relaxer Oil

2 drops cedar

2 drops cypress

2 drops lavender

1 drop lemon grass

Protection Oil 1

1/8 cup jojoba or almond

5 drops black pepper

4 drops petitgrain

1 drop clove

Protection Oil 2

2 drops bergamot

2 drops black pepper

2 drops clove

Protection Oil 3

2 drops cypress

2 drops geranium

2 drops juniper

Protection Oil 4

3 drops palmarosa
4 drops patchouli
2 drops geranium

Protection Oil 5

4 drops patchouli
2 drops palmarosa
3 drops geranium

Protection Oil 6

3 drops black pepper
4 drops patchouli
3 drops bergamot

Protection Oil 7

3 drops cypress
3 drops juniper
3 drops neroli

Protection Oil 8

2 drops palmarosa
5 drops juniper
1 drop geranium

Purification Oil 1

1 drop geranium
1 drop frankincense
1 drop rosemary

Purification Oil 2

2 drops camphor
2 drops cinnamon
2 drops eucalyptus

Purification Oil 3

3 drops grapefruit
4 drops juniper
3 drops lavender

Purification Oil 4

3 drops lavender
2 drops lemon grass
2 drops lemon verbena

Purification Oil 5

3 drops neroli
2 drops orange
2 drops peppermint

Purification Oil 6

3 drops pine
4 drops lavender
2 drops lemon grass

Purification Oil 7

3 drops grapefruit
3 drops lemon grass
3 drops orange

Purification Oil 8

2 drops peppermint
2 drops lemon verbena
2 drops camphor

Purification Oil 9

2 drops peppermint
2 drops eucalyptus
1 drop camphor
4 drops cinnamon

Purification Oil 10

1 drop camphor
1 drop cinnamon

1 drop eucalyptus
1 drop lavender
1 drop lemon grass
1 drop lemon verbena
1 drop lime
1 drop neroli
1 drop orange
1 drop peppermint
1 drop pine

Truth Oil

2 drops patchouli
2 drops honeysuckle
1 drop sage
1 drop balm of Gilead

INCENSE

Beauty Incense

1 cup catnip
3 cups rose

Celibacy Incense

3 cups camphor
2 cups marjoram
1 cup lavender

Circle Invocation Incense

3 cups frankincense
2 cups myrrh
1 cup cinnamon
1 cup mint
1 cup rosemary
1 cup sandalwood

Courage Incense 1

1 cup thyme
1 cup yarrow
1 cup clove
1 cup fennel

Courage Incense 2

2 cups black pepper
1 cup ginger

1 cup onion
3 cups sweet pea

Dream Incense 1

2 cups calendula
2 cups jasmine
1 cup mimosa

Dream Incense 2

3 cups mimosa
3 cups jasmine
1 cup mugwort

Fire Incense

2 cups oak sawdust
3 cups frankincense
1 cup crushed juniper berries
4 drops orange oil
1 cup rosemary

Happiness Incense 1

1 cup apple blossom
1 cup sweet pea
1 cup water lily

Happiness Incense 2

1 cup neroli
2 cups orange
3 cups apple blossom

Happiness Incense 3

1 cup basil
1 cup bergamot
1 cup neroli

Happiness Incense 4

3 cups apple blossom
2 cups orange
1 cup water lily
2 cups sweet pea

Healing Incense 1

1 cup clove
2 cups cypress
2 cups hops
2 cups pine

Healing Incense 2

3 cups eucalyptus
1 cup sandalwood
2 cups spearmint
1 cup coriander

Healing Incense 3

3 cups myrrh
2 cups spearmint
1 cup clove
2 cups cypress

Healing Incense 4

3 cups carnation
2 cups pine
4 cups garlic

Healing Incense 5

3 cups lemon
3 cups lavender
3 cups garlic

Healing Incense 6

3 cups garlic

3 cups clove

4 cups cypress

2 cups lavender

1 cup carnation

1 cup spearmint

Healing Incense 7

4 cups eucalyptus

3 cups garlic

3 cups lemon

2 cups lavender

Healing Incense 8

3 cups thyme

3 cups rue

1 cup carnation

2 cups lemon

Love Incense 1

1 cup thyme

1 cup rose petals

3 cups lavender flowers

Love Incense 2

2 cups apple blossom
2 cups carnation
2 cups freesia
2 cups iris

Love Incense 3

2 cups yarrow
2 cups water lily
3 cups vanilla

Love Incense 4

3 cups lavender
2 cups jasmine
1 cup hyacinth
3 cups gardenia

Love Incense 5

3 cups iris
2 cups lemon verbena
4 cups lilac
3 cups vanilla

Love Incense 6

2 cups cardamom
2 cups coriander
2 cups freesia
2 cups ginger

Love Incense 7

2 cups hyacinth
2 cups jasmine
2 cups lemon verbena
2 cups meadowsweet

Love Incense 8

2 cups narcissus
3 cups plumeria
4 cups rosemary
2 cups iris

Love Incense 9

5 cups vanilla
3 cups tuberose
4 cups ylang-ylang
3 cups lilac

Love Incense 10

1 cup apple blossom
1 cup rosemary
3 cups lavender
2 cups lilac

Magickal Energy Incense 1

2 cups bay
3 cups carnation
2 cups ginger
3 cups nutmeg

Magickal Energy Incense 2

4 cups vanilla
3 cups ginger
3 cups nutmeg

Magickal Energy Incense 3

3 cups orange
3 cups bay
3 cups pine

Magickal Energy Incense 4

4 cups carnation
3 cups pine
2 cups orange

Meditation Incense 1

2 cups frankincense
2 cups rosemary
2 cups sage
2 cups cinnamon
2 cups sandalwood

Meditation Incense 2

2 cups chamomile
3 cups frankincense
2 cups sandalwood

Meditation Incense 3

3 cups myrrh
3 cups frankincense
2 cups chamomile

Memory Incense 1

1 cup clove
3 cups sage
2 cups coriander

Memory Incense 2

3 cups rosemary
3 cups lily of the valley
1 cup sage

Peace Incense 1

2 cups apple blossom
2 cups bergamot
2 cups chamomile
2 cups catnip

Peace Incense 2

3 cups freesia
4 cups gardenia
2 cups white ginger
3 cups jasmine

Peace Incense 3

3 cups jasmine
3 cups lavender
3 cups lily
3 cups lily of the valley

Peace Incense 4

4 cups rose
2 cups ylang-ylang
3 cups lavender
3 cups freesia

Peace Incense 5

5 cups apple blossom
2 cups water lily
3 cups lavender
2 cups jasmine

Peace Incense 6

3 cups marjoram
4 cups lemon balm
3 cups chamomile
4 cups bergamot

Peace Incense 7

4 cups catnip
4 cups lemon balm
4 cups lily of the valley
3 cups freesia

Perfect Mate Incense

3 cups sandalwood
2 cups patchouli
1 cup orrisroot
1 cup dragon's blood
1 cup lemon grass

Physical Energy Incense 1

2 cups bay
2 cups black pepper
3 cups camphor
3 cups caraway

Physical Energy Incense 2

5 cups carnation
4 cups cinnamon
3 cups patchouli
4 cups saffron

Physical Energy Incense 3

2 cups nutmeg
2 cups black pepper
2 cups garlic
2 cups cinnamon

Physical Energy Incense 4

3 cups vanilla
2 cups orange
3 cups lime

Physical Energy Incense 5

5 cups pennyroyal
4 cups pine
3 cups saffron
2 cups bay

Physical Energy Incense 6

2 cups bay
2 cups patchouli
4 cups ginger
3 cups caraway

Physical Energy Incense 7

4 cups black pepper
3 cups camphor
3 cups ginger
2 cups carnation

Prosperity Incense

3 cups bergamot
4 cups cinnamon
4 cups honeysuckle

Protection Incense 1

3 cups basil
3 cups vetivert
3 cups black pepper
3 cups pine

Protection Incense 2

2 cups clove
3 cups pennyroyal
3 cups cumin
3 cups peppermint

Protection Incense 3

2 cups garlic
2 cups cumin
3 cups parsley
2 cups clove

Protection Incense 4

3 cups onion
3 cups cumin
2 cups garlic
1 cup parsley

Psychic Awareness Incense 1

1 cup bay
1 cup celery
1 cup cereus

Psychic Awareness Incense 2

2 cups cinnamon
2 cups iris
3 cups lemon grass
4 cups mace

Psychic Awareness Incense 3

1 cup yarrow
1 cup anise
1 cup nutmeg
1 cup mugwort

Psychic Awareness Incense 4

2 cups celery
3 cups cinnamon
3 cups lemon grass
2 cups nutmeg

Purification Incense 1

4 cups bay
3 cups camphor
2 cups dill
3 cups eucalyptus

Purification Incense 2

3 cups garlic
4 cups dill
2 cups lilac
2 cups hyssop

Purification Incense 3

3 cups hyssop
1 cup eucalyptus
3 cups juniper
1 cup lemon verbena

Purification Incense 4

1 cup orange
1 cup pine
2 cups lime
3 cups neroli

Purification Incense 5

1 cup lemon
1 cup lemon grass
1 cup lemon verbena
1 cup lemon balm
1 cup lime

Purification Incense 6

1 cup tulip
1 cup bay
1 cup dill
3 cups garlic

Purification Incense 7

4 cups dill
1 cup lemon verbena
2 cups garlic
2 cups ginger

Purification Incense 8

3 cups juniper
2 cups lilac
4 cups lime

Sex Incense 1

1 cup ginger
2 cups vanilla
1 cup jasmine

Sex Incense 2

1 cup jasmine
2 cups vanilla
1 cup sandalwood

Sex Incense 3

2 cups rose
1 cup vanilla
1 cup ylang-ylang

Sex Incense 4

2 cups patchouli
1 cup ginger
2 cups vanilla

Sleep Incense 1

1 cup bergamot
1 cup chamomile
1 cup celery

Sleep Incense 2

2 cups hops
2 cups marjoram
2 cups hyacinth

Sleep Incense 3

2 cups bergamot
4 cups lavender
3 cups jasmine

Sleep Incense 4

2 cups chamomile
2 cups hyacinth
4 cups lavender

BATH SALTS

Venus Bath Salts (love spell)

1 cup salt
4 drops rose
4 drops musk
8 drops jasmine
4 drops lavender

Fantasy Bath Salts (love spell)

1 cup salt
8 drops honeysuckle
8 drops rose
4 drops patchouli

Circle of Flame Bath Salts (love spell)

1 cup salt
4 drops musk
8 drops violet
4 drops rose

High Priestess Bath Salts

1 cup salt
8 drops wisteria

8 drops lavender

4 drops rose

Spirit Blessings Bath Salts

1 cup salt

8 drops violet

4 drops ylang-ylang

8 drops wisteria

4 drops sandalwood

Prosperity Bath Salts 1

1 cup salt

8 drops lotus

2 drops cinnamon

8 drops sandalwood

3 drops myrrh

2 drops allspice

Prosperity Bath Salts 2

1 cup salt

8 drops myrrh

3 drops cinnamon

8 drops sandalwood

3 drops allspice

Fire Lust Bath Salts

1 cup epsom salt
1/2 cup sea salt
1/2 cup baking soda
14 drops orange
14 drops lime
10 drops rosemary
5 drops cinnamon

Aphrodite's Bath Salts

1 cup epsom salt
1/2 cup sea salt
1/2 cup baking soda
4 drops lavender
6 drops violet
7 drops jasmine

Moon magick Bath Salts

1 cup salt
8 drops sandalwood
1/8 tsp. orrisroot
8 drops lotus

Section 13

Incantations

Air/Wind Spell 1

With this intent the magick I dare
To send out the element of air.
The magick I cast this spell I'll see,
This is my will, so mote it be.

Air/Wind Spell 2

With this intent I call to Air
To cast my spell to the winds so fair,
And bring my heart's desire to me.
This is my will, so mote it be.

Beauty 1

Oh Goddess,
Help me to see
The beauty that resides within me.
Bring this beauty out of its shell,
To the surface where it may dwell.
This is my wish, so mote it be.

Beauty 2

Moon above,
Full and bright,
Enhance my beauty
With all your might.
Grant me this blessing,
I ask of you.
This is my wish
For beauty true.

Beauty 3 (for use with oil)

Oh Goddess,
I stand here in your guardian light,
Empower this oil with your might.
The gift of beauty is what I ask,
Please accept this as your task.
This is my will, so mote it be.

Beauty 4

Beauty seen,
Pure and true,
Is the gift
I ask from you.

Beauty 5

Grant me beauty,
Grant me grace,
Grant me this wish
For a beautiful face
For others to see
As I do too.
Grant me this wish
For beauty true.

Business Success 1

Oh Goddess,
Help me to see
The path to take
For a future bright.
Grant me this with your guiding light.

Business Success 2

Moon above,
Full and bright,
Show me the way
With your guiding light

To make my future
Plans come true.
Grant me this blessing,
I ask of you.

Business Success 3

Water, fire, earth, and air,
My success is in your care.
Show me guidance
To choose my path.
Decisions I make
Must be right.
Help me with your loving light.

Business Success 4

My need is great,
My heart is true,
My future success
I ask from you.
Fulfill this wish sent to thee,
Work this magick just for me.

Business Success 5 (for use with oil)

Oh Goddess,
I stand here in your guardian light,
Empower this oil with your might.
Business success is what I ask,
Please accept this as your task.
This is my will,
So mote it be.

Celibacy (for virgins)

Oh Goddess,
Grant me the strength
To keep my body
And virginity safe
And not give in to
Temptations path.

Courage 1

Oh Goddess,
Help me to be
Courageous and brave
In my time of need.

This is my wish,
So mote it be.

Courage 2

With the intent to make me brave
I ask for the courage that I do crave.
Give me the will, strength, and power
To face my fears in my darkest hour.

Courage 3

Oh Goddess,
Help me to see
The courage that resides within me.
Bring this trait out of its shell,
To the surface where it may dwell.

Courage 4

Moon above,
Full and bright,
Show me the way
With your guiding light.
Give me courage,
Make me brave and true.

This is the blessing
I ask from you.

Courage 5

Give me strength,
Oh Goddess strong,
To help me detect
Right from wrong.
Give me the courage,
Oh moon of bright,
To face the challenges
That I must fight.

Dreams 1

Oh Goddess,
Help me to see
The deep, true
Meaning of my dreams.

Dreams 2

Moon above,
Full and bright,

Give me the gift
Of dream insight.

Dreams 3 (for use with oil)

Oh Goddess,
I stand here in your guardian light,
Empower this oil with your might.
Clarity of my dreams is what I ask,
Please accept this as your task.

Dreams 4

Insight, clearness and clarity,
Grant these gifts of three to me.
To interpret my dreams and
Find what they mean,
To know what my dreams
Are telling me.

Dreams 5

Visions are gifts from the Goddess above,
To help us learn to deal with love,
With what affects us day by day,

And choose the path for which we were made.
Grant me the gift of sight to see
What my dreams aren't meant to be.

Earth Spell

Into this soil through my hand,
My intent I do command.
Make it last,
Make it strong,
From earth to me where it belongs.

Fire Spell

Element of fire burning bright,
I call you here with me tonight.
Fulfill this desire sent to thee,
Work this magick just for me.

Happiness 1 (for use with oil)

Oh Goddess,
I stand here in your guardian light,
Empower this oil with your might.
The gift of happiness is what I ask,
Please accept this as your task.

Happiness 2

Moon above,
Full and bright,
Grant me happiness
This magickal night.

Happiness 3

Pleasure, joy, delight, and bliss,
Oh dear Goddess, grant me this.

Happiness 4

Oh my Goddess,
Blessed be.
Happiness and ecstasy,
Are the gifts I ask from thee.

Happiness 5

Grant me contentment,
Happiness, and peace
To serve my days with
Beauty and grace.
With love from above,
And all around,

My heart overflows with
The joy I have found.

Healing 1 (for use with oil)

Oh Goddess,
I stand here in your guardian light,
Empower this oil with your might.
The gift of healing is what I ask,
Please accept this as your task.

Healing 2

Moon above,
Full and bright,
Grant me good health
This magickal night.

Healing 3

Oh Goddess,
Instill these herbs
With your healing grace,
To relieve my illness
And infuse my faith.

Healing 4

Heal what ails me,
Cure my illness.
Make my body and
Soul whole and one again.
Return my strength,
Build my immunity.
Make my body and
Soul whole and one again.

Healing 5

Oh Goddess grant me this.
Sickness will end and
Health return.
Heal me now,
Illness is gone,
My suffering is eased.
Let my sickness
Now be purged.

Love 1

The love I want,
The love I need,

Let it be returned to me.
This is my wish
So mote it be.

Love 2

Moon above,
Full and bright,
Find my love
This (spring, summer, autumn, winter) night.
Send my love,
True and dear,
And bring my
Match closer near.

Love 3

Oh Goddess,
Bring unto me
A love so simple,
Easy, and free.
A love that is ready, true, and right,
For this I wish with all my might.
So mote it be.

Love 4

Water, fire, earth, and air,
My heart is in need of loving care.
Find my soul mate,
Caring and true,
A perfect match of love from you.
This is my wish,
So mote it be.

Love 5

Moon above,
Full and bright,
Grant me love
This magickal night.

Magickal Energy 1 (for use with oil)

Oh Goddess,
I stand here in your guardian light,
Empower this oil with your might.
The gift of magickal energy is what I ask,
Please accept this as your task.

Magickal Energy 2

Moon above,
Full and bright,
Grant me energy
This magickal night.

Magickal Energy 3

Grant me the power
To cast my spells
And make my desires
Come true.
Grant me the knowledge
To cast my spells
With true intent.
Grant me the strength
To use my power
And knowledge,
And walk only
In the white light.

Magickal Energy 4

Fingers to the heavens
I stretch out,

And ask the Goddess to fill me
With her loving light.
Give me strength,
Give me power,
Give me energy.
Of this I ask thee, Goddess,
So mote it be.

Magickal Energy 5

Charge me, oh Goddess,
With the energy I
Need to work my
Spells so magickally.
(repeat three times)
This is my will,
So mote it be.

Meditation 1

Oh Goddess,
Grant me peace and tranquility
To meditate safely
And grow in my spirituality.

Meditation 2

One with peace,
One with tranquility,
One with nature.
Let your spirit
Flow through my
Thoughts and clear
My mind of
Rambling thoughts
And useless clutter.
Open my mind,
Open my mind,
Open my mind.

Meditation 3

Release my mind
From its burden
Of thought and
Let the ideas run free.
(repeat 3 times)

Meditation 4

Open my heart,
Push all else
To the back or
To the side.
Let love and light
And life
Flow.
Let peace and calm reside.
Let love and light
And life
Flow.

Meditation 5

Oh Goddess,
Grant me clarity.
Oh Goddess,
Grant me purity.
Oh Goddess,
Grant me serenity.
This is my will,
So mote it be.

Memory 1 (for use with oil)

Oh Goddess,
I stand here in your guardian light,
Empower this oil with your might.
A better memory is what I ask,
Please accept this as your task.

Memory 2

Moon above,
Full and bright,
Help my memory
This magickal night.

Memory 3

Fill my mind
With what it needs
Always to remember.
(repeat 3 times)
This is my wish,
So mote it be.

Memory 4

Goddess of night,
Moon so bright,

Boost my memory skills.
Help me recall long ago,
As if it were just now.

Money 1 (for use with oil)

Oh Goddess,
I stand here in your guardian light,
Empower this oil with your might.
The gift of money is what I ask,
Please accept this as your task.

Money 2

Moon above,
Full and bright,
Bring me money
This magickal night.

Peace 1 (for use with oil)

Oh Goddess,
I stand here in your guardian light,
Empower this oil with your might.
The gift of peace is what I ask,
Please accept this as your task.

Peace 2

Moon above,
Full and bright,
Grant me peace
This magickal night.

Physical Energy 1 (for use with oil)

Oh Goddess,
I stand here in your guardian light,
Empower this oil with your might.
Physical energy is what I ask,
Please accept this as your task.

Physical Energy 2

Moon above,
Full and bright,
Grant me energy
This magickal night.

Protection 1 (for use with oil)

I stand here in your guardian light,
Empower this oil with your might.

Protection from harm is what I ask,
Please accept this as your task.

Protection 2

Moon above,
Full and bright,
Grant me protection
This magickal night.

Protection 3

Protect me with your guiding light,
Oh Goddess of strength, day and night.

Protection 4

By the Full Moon's light,
I call to thee.
To use your might,
I conjure thee
With all you see,
To protect my home,
My family, and me.

Protection 5

Hail fair Moon Goddess,
Ruler of the night,
Guard me and mine,
Until the daylight.

Psychic Awareness 1 (for use with oil)

Oh Goddess,
I stand here in your guardian light,
Empower this oil with your might.
Psychic awareness is what I ask,
Please accept this as your task.

Psychic Awareness 2

Moon above,
Full and bright,
Grant me awareness
This magickal night.

Psychic Awareness 3
(for use with candle)

I set to fire the inner light,
So I may see with my second sight.

I empower this candle to shine the way,
To show me the future to see what lay.
Spirits of air flow through me,
Pass through me with psychic energy.

Purification 1 (for use with oil)

Oh Goddess,
I stand here in your guardian light,
Empower this oil with your might.
Purification is what I ask,
Please accept this as your task.

Purification 2

Moon above,
Full and bright,
Grant me purity
This magickal night.

Sex 1 (for use with oil)

Oh Goddess,
I stand here in your guardian light,
Empower this oil with your might.

The gift of sex is what I ask,
Please accept this as your task.

Sex 2

Venus, mighty Goddess of lust,
I call upon you and pledge my trust,
To bring me closer to my heart's desire,
And quench my thirst with burning fire.

Sleep 1 (for use with oil)

Oh Goddess,
I stand here in your guardian light,
Empower this oil with your might.
The gift of sleep is what I ask,
Please accept this as your task.

Sleep 2

Moon above,
Full and bright,
Grant me sleep
This magickal night.

Truth 1 (for use with oil)

Oh Goddess,
I stand here in your guardian light,
Empower this oil with your might.
The gift of truth is what I ask,
Please accept this as your task.

Truth 2

Moon above,
Full and bright,
Grant me truth
This magickal night.

Casting the Circle

Three times round I cast my blade,
That this Circle shall be made.
Sacred space within this Circle now lies,
Protected from unwelcome eyes.
Let no one enter here within,
Who has not been made welcome,
So mote it be.

Opening the Circle

The Circle is open, but unbroken.
Merry meet, merry part, and
Merry meet again.

Section 14

Worksheets

Spells

Spell name:

Type of spell:

Date created:

Time created (Specific or general):

Specific purpose:

Ingredients/Supplies:

Location required:

Moon phase required:

Deities invoked:

Step by step instructions:

Additional notes:

Dates and times performed, along with results:

Rituals

Ritual name:

Type of ritual:

Date created:

Time created (Specific or general):

Moon phase required:

Astrological correspondence required:

Specific purpose:

Tools and other items required:

Deities invoked:

Approximate length of ritual:

Ritual composition:

Additional notes:

Dates and times performed, along with results:

Bibliography

Brier, Bob. *Ancient Egyptian Magic: Spells, Incantations, Potions, Stories and Rituals.* New York: Quill, 1981.

Bruce, Marie. *Candle Burning Rituals.* London: Quantum, 2001.

Conway, D.J. *Moon Magick: Myth & Magic, Crafts and Recipes, Rituals & Spells.* St.Paul, Minn: Lewellyn, 2002.

Cunningham, Scott. *Magical Aromatherapy: The Power of Scent.* St Paul, Minn: Lewellyn, 2000.

Franklin, Anna. *Midsummer: Magical Celebrations of the Summer Solstice.* St Paul, Minn: Lewellyn, 2002.

Galenorn, Yasmine. *Embracing the Moon: A Witch's Guide to Ritual Spellcraft and Shadow Work.* Minn: Lewellyn, 2001.

Harris, Eleanor. *Ancient Egyptian Divination and Magic.* York Beach, Maine: Samual Weiser, Inc., 1998.

McCoy, Edain. *Ostara: Customs, Spells and Rituals for the Rites of Spring.* Minn: Lewellyn, 2002.

Pepper, Elizabeth. *The Witches Almanac Spring 2002 to Spring 2003.* Newport Publishers. 2002

Regula, DeTraci. *The Mysteris of Isis, Her Worship and Magick.* Minn: Lewellyn, 2001.

Zimmerman, Denise and Gleason, Katherine. *The Complete Idiots Guide to Wicca and Witchcraft.* Indianapolis: Alpha Books, 2000.

Index

About the Author

Kerri Connor dances under the moon in a rural area of Illinois with her husband, three children, four stepchildren, her dog Foxy and cat Quantico. She is an avid reader, loves gardening, and is a die-hard Chicago Bears fan.